Wen Kroy

hey

Shela Blacks interesting all of the books of poetry, War Brood

unlike
The New York al

which is an inverted
the words of New York

was reminisce
Inverted version
2 words used to

New York
26 J. 193
02
But differe
Kroy Wen

on 20 July 1931 when
The NewYorker the article
a Kroy Wen is use the words
New York

The logic behind This invention then as a draw
so to always so dead or own use the big apple. Sheila's P
poetically
uses New York is a American
many aspects

Wen Kroy

Sheila Black

Dream Horse Press
Aptos, California

To Mo,
fellow poet
friend!
Thanks for all

Dream Horse Press
Post Office Box 2080, Aptos, California 95001-2080

Wen Kroy Copyright © 2014 Sheila Black

Printed in the United States of America
Published in 2014 by Dream Horse Press

ISBN 978-1-935716-26-6

Cover artwork:

Meteorology
by Michele Marcoux

www.michelemarcoux.com

For my daughters Annabelle and Eliza Hayse
For my friends—Michele Marcoux, Lynne Thermann, and Connie Voisine

TABLE OF CONTENTS

Wen Kroy

Expiration Date

This is the season to recommit ourselves
to making grow what we can. The soil is packed
hard; we break a sweat trying to prepare it
for the seeds, we stab holes into the
dirt and each time we drop one in
faith seems slighter even than mustard seed.
More like the blown head of the dandelion
which bends down and gives its all. This is
the season for giving up the stories we
have repeated through the long dark of who
did what to who. What would be a world
without history? It would be this patch of
yard, scraped by March wind and rain,
bare and nascent. Already the crickets are
arriving from their birth-beds under the earth.
The grackles have claimed this patch as their
own. The small wars, now in abeyance, stir
again among the silent, the meek. I know we
will miss the first blooming, but I mark it
for you here, on this page. Look, you wake
into the world, and the trees are all adorned.
If this is not for you, then who is it for?

Broken World

(for Grandmaster Flash)

On the streets we find needles and
soda cans, bags slashed in bright red
shaking in the wind. And when the train
rocks by there are names, which at a distance
look like magnolia or barbed wire, tags
that move like sound on the eye. Perhaps
it begins by him thinking about how nothing
is clean, virgin, untouched. He does
not know this is what he thinks. Only
that when he tries to be still inside himself
he is conscious of that swelling, pieces
of voices: scraps, leaves, squares of broken glass.
He scrubs his little cousin's highchair
until the kitchen is dark and still the tracks
of marks. Fork-tines. spilled food.

Soon he is breaking into the vacant
lots, limboing under the electric fences, past
the chained dogs where in the split front seats
of wrecked cars, he dismantles the silent radios
in his lap, chrome boxes bursting with colored
wire, broken hearts out of which he
will build a new body, a machine that will
speak for all of them.

The woman dissolves the sweet pill under
her tongue. Rose petals on eyelids, thick, velvety
stranger in the garden than the birds with
their bead-bright eyes. She can hear the hush
that is the loneliness of the blood in
the body, what it is to discover that boundary,
tauter than the skin on water, tougher,
what seals you. She can remember when she
believed she was sister to the flamboyant tree and
that the garden was *safe for her alone.*
There were ferns ribboned in sienna and umber,
a green like a light cut down the
middle and under all was plum, violet, grape.
By the far wall, the lime trees smelled
of age. In the fountain, the carp rose with their blown
mouths to the surface of the water where
she fed them day-old bread. And deep among
the coffee trees and creeping vines, the pale boy,
sightless statue, shining in the dark. The earth
was made of cinnamon and the age of the leaves and
the day she saw the ants strip the wren bare
in moments; it had broken its wing and they ate
it resolutely, shining lines of them like a miniscule
army. And this all happened in silence.

1.

Listen, he says, *lie on the floor it will be fine.*
He says: *You would be pretty if only you didn't move so much.*

They have to kneel in the gym to see if their
skirts are too short. The teacher checks them with a tape measure.

Her friend in the stall with the cut wrists pleads,
don't tell anyone, don't get any help
but she can't stop it herself—furrowing and pooling
in the cuffs. Raw liver. A washed pink.

What do you want to do a silly thing like that for?

Listen, she tells him, *I think I'm going to be sick.*

2.

The sheaves of daffodils in the
fruit stalls, their green in the mist,
like something cut open, and the crazy woman
who claims she is the sun,
swaddles herself in bits of tablecloth,
crepe brocade from sofas.

3.

Three months gone she goes alone. The room smells of bleach.
The woman behind the desk shouts *youngest first.*
They take the chain from her neck, the bracelet from her wrist.

The bracelet is silver like the moon, and she never
gets it back. *You must be dreaming, girlie. Who would steal
it in a place like this?*

4.

*Sun Woman claws at her face and shrieks. They
will take her away soon because she is a danger to herself
and others. She has dyed all her tablecloths black.*

5.

Once she spies him on the street in his long tweed coat.
She knows his face will freeze if he sees
her, so she walks backwards, crouches in
a doorway.

6.

*Later, she finds a card with two faces of
the moon. One tells the Earth
Your daughter is in hell. The other is the huntress.
She roams the woods with her dogs and
no one escapes.*

7.

Washed pink, raw liver, silver around the wrist.
And the daffodils, their sun-heads dulling.

Once he reached out for her; he was still asleep.
He said *You are here, oh, I'm glad it is you.*

And the moon was in the room, and there were things
she did not notice: a shadow like a sword, the night bird pecking
in the icy soil under the juniper. The Dog Star. A cloud
of frozen dust making tracks in the sky.

Getting Over the Fear of Form

I wanted to go back to *undivided light*,
the bruised stem of the pear,
wasp-body, heat, the slick of green across
the skin, but I wanted these to
endure; I saw already the fly-flit of
years across my territory. Here, my eyes
dimming, skin raddling.
It was the crossing I could not manage.
The notion of what would be left.

The strictures were what would bind me.
I would carve them, leave
what small traces of myself—In the ghazal
the last line must contain the poet's
name. It was not my name I wanted.
It was the outside, the *undivided light*.
Here, the fig, the pomegranate, the
flecked stone. Here, but with my
eyes watching, mouth opening.

Las Dos Fridas or Script for the Erased

As if she was severed from me in the surgery
itself, I immediately began to refer to her in the
third person—the girl, girl-with-the-torqued-
legs, crip girl who was and was not me.
I pictured her peering in windows, apparating
in mirrors. Invisible on any corner. She knew
the color rain makes against smoked glass, blew
bubbles at the fish in their silent aquariums. She
was me before I became so fallen, sneaking
Salem cigarettes with the other girls on the fourth
floor bathroom. Trying so hard to fit in you could
see that desire—a sheen on the skin. The year I
learned to walk again—a wheelchair, crutches, crutches
discarded, and everyone saying it was a miracle,
such a great, great thing, as if I could now
be welcomed into the club of people. A door closed
somewhere, and she was behind it. I pictured her
staring down at her left hand, uncurling the palm
to study the lines. I pictured her building a map, a
way out of this place and back to me. And when I
first saw the painting, *Las Dos Fridas*, their fingers
laced together, the blood line leaking between
them, I knew what that picture meant: *Here she is.*
Look at her. Look at her and love us both.

Ghost Time

(for Evan Childs)

We drove down Rock Creek in the
Buick that swerved sideways,
crashed into all the parked vehicles,
crushed steel, a glitter like
shook foil, your eyes
unreadable behind your
sunglasses, gangster jacket,
red headband crushing your hair.
How to explain the rage of the
dispossessed, why among so much we
felt so hungry—your parents
both lawyers, risen up and out
to what? In the big house
on Northhampton you said *I could
junk everything*, days cutting school,
sex, chocolate, opium distilled
from hearts of lettuces. Of course,
I loved you—worse than any
teenage novel—the way my
heart kept pumping useless,
my breath a flutter, a luna moth.
It was everything we wanted,
but when you kissed my cheek I
traced already the shape of
our decline, brief arabesque,
then the descent to indifference.
Easier to just walk away

but the window, your corner
still draws me. The elm trees would die out
in a few years, but then they fanned out
with their amphora shape—
crackle of worm and seed, the toxic
greens along the highway softening
with spring. Your hand,
the burn of its shape, its cup
against me. I was sure you would grow
weary of us as of every other thing,
but I should have held you anyway—
the two of us so locked in ghost time,
the blur after Southern Comfort or Maker's
Mark, our joy in not knowing
where we ended, the world began.
The taste of you strange
on my tongue. I could have palmed
you like a bright coin; instead I flung you
away as if you were the wish I would
make on eternity. Now you are dead,
and I see what terrible things the living do.
I walk past your house and do not miss a
beat. This forgetting, the complete renunciation
I was already practicing—

Blessing/Blessure

The birth of love like a moth
expanding, wet rag to flower,

the uprising, a light
from every object, even the dust charged.

Then the charred after:
the room when you know they just
don't *like* you anymore.

The one undoes her heart,
and the other frightened
by that terrible engine, pump full
of blood and god-knows-what-else.

First Love

When you drink too early, it is praying.

The silence of Murphy's like churches.

Cigarette smoke and the creased faces.

The stories that lose their luster by 10:00 a.m.

Subways and jobs you show up for that pay by the hour.

In the evenings packed in the express train

like sardine, a woman's swollen hands

clutching the rail. When a jumper jumps

the blue spark fills the tunnel. You have been told

this. You re-tell it even though you suspect

it is not true. The jumper means delays. Passenger

with the knife he threatens to hold to his own

throat. You sigh and ache. Smell the sweat of

other people. Picture the insides of their

brains. A million, two million shell-like buildings.

Complex stairwells that crisscross; rooms with a

limited view. In the apartment you share with the

boyfriend who scares you, a view of airshaft. Two

men kissing in a room lit by televisions. You envy

their tenderness. You are better at faking it. The part

of you he will never touch like a black pearl, a

necrotic gleam. This will kill you. The failure &

the failure though you know the dimensions

of what should be a vast and terrible shining, a listening

like the ears of the recording angels, acute

to the smallest stammer, the mildest declensions.

He gives you a card early one morning when the

streets are grise-pearl with ice, the breath of man-

holes. *Happy (Sad) Valentines*. You know he

knows and still you move through the rooms, boiling

water for tea or noodles, folding his shirts at

the corner Laundromat. How he smells better to you

in the steam of the industrial driers or when not

there. *Someone you could. A life you might.* And

not this ghost-tripping where when he leaves the

apartment, you search his pockets. Not because

you suspect anything, but because, skin

aside, you are uneasy strangers. This smashed

thing you sweep from the floor. This accidental

bruising around your wrists. Pondering the

numbers he has written in matchbooks,

stubs of movie tickets, as if they could provide

you a way to enter, walk in, sit in an armchair by a

window, hear the groaning of trucks, the voices

from outside as he does. All the time your loneliness

like a raincoat pricked with so many holes

that you are always drenched and shivering

with how much there is to take in.

This Slow Ache Within Music

(for Billy Bang)

By the tenement window the blue light thick
        as spider silk Billy is playing again
for me the violin's wretched sobbing the whine
        that breaks into high curved glass
rise on the window sill glasses of water tainted
        with his blood cigarettes burning away in
his fingers. This is a lullaby this is a medicine for
        sleep. Outside in the hall a dreamer walks down
the stairs the backs of other people are menacing
        the puddle turns to an eye. God watches everywhere
written in us shame and grief and the perfect
        note which swells and rises over the dumpsters
and streetlights over the cracked bottles and the
        cracked pipe where the children sell *Montana*
and *Danger.* Billy plays for me the bone at the
        center of this ache where the cells keep
circling and multiplying white plates red suns we
        are walking among the silent lost crush where
the city opens itself to us like a struck bell a stoked furnace.

The Readers

(for Andrew)

We had no couch, no chairs, only
a few wooden crates from
the Greek fruit market on Broadway,

raw pine spattered with the
juice of peaches and grapes. Only
the mattress we set on the

floor and the floors smeared
blood crimson, the blue of the
Aegean. The plexiglass front window

with its streaks like glue. Below
the view of fire escapes and
concrete-poured stoops where

Mr. Rodriguez and Junior sat
downing bottles of El Presidente,
concealed in crushed paper

bags. And the summer smell of
fruit in decay, the whoosh of
exploded firecrackers, the

chemical burn of crack from the
basement. And we had our books,
lined in crooked stacks against

the rough walls, filling the short
hallway, on top of the medicine cabinet:
New Dimensions paperbacks from

the sixties, the pages cracking
and yellow. The austere green leather
of Modern Library, the noirs

with their bright covers, creases
and stains, bad girls on stairways
like the one in our building,

dank with oil, smell of pork roast and
cigarettes. The rows of words we ran our
eyes over, our fingers across as if

they were the bread we could
eat and so live by, words and more words
tendrilling around us like the vines

from some exotic orchid or the humble
wisteria, the bleeding hearts, for
what else can I call it—that flooding in,

that sweetness? Coming home from work,
packed into the train like lentil seed,
the express diving from local, and

the sentences sifting in through our
narrowed eyes, reaching to flick
the pages as the stations roared by.

All the holy names we chanted like
the Rosicrucians or early Gnostics,
believing we could find the God above

the false gods who ruled us. Rimbaud
and Mallarme, *Stop Time* and
The Story of the Rose. I can hardly

bear to ponder the life of them inside me—the
words rolling over, and behind a soft
explosion that kept shooting sparks,

the feasts of them laid out on our
bare tables, so that we moved through,
rapt and unseeing as the ancient

ecstatics, building the ghost cities
that grew ever more densely
populated, the voices that arched up and

through, leaking across our
railway apartment, the flooded pipes,
the bathtubs brimming. How could we

even see what was in front of us—
Junior dead and Mr. Rodriguez grieving,
novels we had not yet learned

to translate.

Goodwill

Objects matter though we try to pretend
otherwise. For instance, in this thin gray
gabardine with bone buttons, I am the woman
with the backcombed hair who stands
at the back of the bar listening to Billie
on the useless jukebox sing of "clear
day" and "empty road," or now in the brown
windbreaker, flecked with distemper paint,
I am the girl at the highway rest-stop,
stranded, and no one stops. I am looking for
you in the pockets of the coats; each time
I put in my hand, a small cool moist that
might be you, but isn't. And the shoes
of the dead don't fit, my feet slide out,
slippery, stocking-footed to dabble in the
dust. The boiled sweaters in colors like
candy, racks and racks of them. What home-
coming game, what Saturday night date? I
keep thinking of wars and empires—the
burning house and what I would save. If
this was a postcard, I would write simply
I miss you and a row of exclamation points,
xs and os like some primitive numbering.
I pay $2.95 for a zebra-collared black
velvet jacket. It hugs itself around me.
The pockets are sewn shut, even so
I keep trying to unravel them.

Muse

At times myself as on a heraldic
tapestry. My own heart
in my lap like some terrible
red baby. And you behind, a
falcon at your wrist, the beak
bent as though it might drink
from you as from a stream.
At times, myself as in a tower,
the woman who hides
her lover in a cage. He is a
black bird who sings the moon.
And she does not know how
to live without him. She sprinkles
lime on the fields, and he is
frozen, and then he fades. At times
myself, the woman after,
stitching. A white thread on
a cloth of snow, a raven
thread on a belt of ebony.
Whatever she makes vanishing
like rain. Absence I rehearse
through your palpable indifference,
as though you gifted me with
an infinite against which to hone my
ideas of mortal, or of what it
takes to love. The heart on the
tapestry in gilt thread, dry to

the touch, a frigid immaculate
bearing us as all beauties bear us (as on
horseback) from this world of
things, *cold, hoof, sod, breathing.*

At the Embajada

When we felt weak we ate monfongo,
the high-piled sandcastle plates of plantain
mashed with pork cracklings. On Sunday mornings
the plantanos maduros like coins
of Spanish gold—that starched sweetness,
café con leche any time at all with
the small pale slices of fried bread. In winter,
ropa vieja—used clothes—the shredded
meat mixed with the gravy of peppers, onions,
tomatoes. Sandwiches Cubanos always,
flat and steaming, marked with the iron bars
of the grill. We ate hungover and lovesick.
We ate when they were still sluicing the blood-
from-the-night-before from the sidewalks. We
ate beside the old married couples, the suicidal
teens, the gangbangers, and addicts. We ate
greedily; we ate out of need. We ate as we were
splitting—table partitioned with our terrible endings,
the sudden arcana, stretched silence. We ate
as we had once eaten when it was all new—
in thrall to the city—the burst hydrants, the
dazzled sluicing of a world. We ate as the girl
behind the counter wept unceasing—the
rent had gone up; they could no longer afford the
lease. We ate flan with burnt caramel spilling
around the saucer at the bottom. Drank the
imported beer from the back of the menu,

grass-green bottles of ice-cold El Presidente—
the dictator with his white moustaches, the
benevolent but menacing glimmer in his eye.
We ate ourselves into history, plate after plate
like the great paintings in the museums—
grease gilded with achiote, the bone starch of
yucca, the roots and the organs splayed,
dismembered. We ate carelessly, we ate with relish,
as our lives turned and burned, we ordered, we ate.

Icon

Your roommate we never saw,
instead holing ourselves in your bedroom, a gray
newsprint light of airshafts,

the icon of Jerome on the far wall,
gilded ebony weight, stories of
your grandmother injecting herself daily

with insulin, the vein in her
worn thigh, still strong beneath her
support-hose, nylons held up

with safety pins, your tenderness for
her arrangements, the luxury of
blood on a finger, pool darkening:

scarlet, ebony, scarlet. White nights
beside you, the ache of a love
that was not sexual but more

brotherly, or so you said, finger tracing
the line of my throat, the hollow
of the voice box, swooping goblet

of the clavicle. On the phone, the junkie
whisper, "Are you okay?" so much
freight in three simple words.

The Poloroids you took of me, facing
the mirror beside your closet, a
peering-in you recognized. *Tell me*

only your name/my name. So often I
was your grandmother again, fleeing
from Izmir, the exodus from Turkey—

a hundred years, a buried massacre,
the ships of Piraeus, a smell of dun oysters,
seaweed and barnacle, clinging.

In the groceries of Pittsburgh, the diners
under the bridges, flavors diluted,
and the astonishing distillation of

sorrow, a taste that flooded the back of
our throats, each time we shot up.
White nights and fans and susurrus

of traffic—cargo human and otherwise,
an epic of multiple displacements,
the lovers who lived in the mirror

or around the next corner. Your roommate
treading lightly in from his night-
waiter job to surprise me one night

in the bathroom tub, cream princess
dress pulled down over my shoulders,
a mottle of bruises, his brief

pity so thoroughly mingled with disgust;
melon slant of light snapping away
as he shut the door and the dull

thud of music from your room—
Lou Reed singing about his high
school football coach, the

battering of bodies as if there was
something to break through or into,
you, putting your fingers to

my wrist, a delicacy that undid me.

Nocturne Avenue D

Like sugar on the tongue
but bitter, the curve of light
in the tenement room, a
confusion of moons, even
the sound bent by brick,
stone, the tap which drips
irregularly, each droplet
clutching the errant light—

Beautiful what you find in
the almost silences–the pauses
in street sound like caught
breath, and still you write
me a history of how you
fell in love with slow death:
The filmy packets,
child-candy colors, stamped,
*Moosehead, Buffalo, The
Bones*, the woman who hides them
in the broken pipe just lying on the
street, the children who scatter out
eye-level in front of the cars,
that rush of whisper—

Midnight, 7th and D, white amaryllis,
bruises blooming on your skin,
a trace of the great hush

within, the blood unreeling like
a slow snake through
grassy hills and that first time
when the world turned all ear,
a shell opening around you:
a ruby ticking, the insistent
track of the heart.

Wen Kroy

For the show there was Hamlet and
John Dufresne and you, painting
on the backs of doors, the pieces of
the dismantled organ from down the street.
And that guy—he was just
a janitor from a nearby basement,
carrying a hollow cardboard
tube. No one knew what to do

with him. We offered to buy him beer or
a vodka-and-tonic, but he said he
didn't drink. Not anymore. And I am
passing over the stories within
stories: Lynn the red-headed bar-
tender, who said you were the kind
of guy she might kiss and forget in
the morning. And I always thought
you did kiss her, in the black-painted
bathroom, grimed glass, silver-
scarred letters, couples that didn't make it,
some girl calling some other girl

"You slag whore." And a bar like that
can be a secret world, always nightfall,
whenever you enter, the clock on
the wall never reading precisely right,
so that we, too, felt, we might stretch

out into some other space
or time. Up all night, feeling the burn of
our throats, faces painted and
repainted by passing cars. He held
the tube right up close. There is no
simple way to help this story escape.
It lives in the tunnel which smells of paper.

When the show was going up, Lynn
cleared off the bar. And he pulled out
the reams of crackling draftsman
paper, translucent, chequered
with sky-blue lines.

Wen Kroy, he said, was where we lived
now and forever, alongside this city,
the one where his daughter died, hit by
a yellow cab. The streets moving
in reverse direction, the buildings even, the
same but subtly rearranged. He had only
reached as far as East 7th, rising up
from the Hudson, block at a time. Eternity
to trace the span of the bridges, the slow
ooze of the polluted river, which, too,
flowed in the opposite direction—a kind of
mirror, bizarre, incandescent.

The bar time did not change. The walls
did not resolve into any other shape, much as I
wished it. And in our tenement, a hundred
blocks north, the painting count kept
rising—battered wood and stray bits of
canvas, cardboard squares propped

against walls, covering floors. Base
pigments. Red. Yellow. Blue. Cars and
streetlights—what rushes up and
through. Your madness like a reflection

in the simple knife used to slice
bread, the ordinary—the way it shimmers
uncontrollable at the edge of
perception. And I didn't love you. I
didn't love you anymore.

Little Grief

I feed you warm milk from a dropper. All night
whinge and moan.

You make a lousy guest—shred the furniture,
piss on the rug.

The neighbors gaze at you askance, but I can't
stop listening to you whistle in and out,

like the conversation the river has with itself as night
burbles on and on, song

that might almost be a silence—large as a gift, sparkly
as a tree in ice

(and why do I believe chill makes the world a glass?).

I resist believing in the accident of origin—the grain
in the shell around which a shimmering globe takes form,

but I can picture so clearly the mess of your birth,
the floor of straw, the slick around

a body. Why I clutch at you, my purse of pens,
my sack of ash.

Little Grief, little grief. Who is ever cherished enough?

Hurricane Day

They said we should tape the windows;
store candles and water, on no account go to
work or ride the subway. Lights out. And
the sky that morning through the tenement

windows—a greeny yellow, a dangerous light,
but muted as sound in a snowstorm, a bandage
wrapped around the suddenly slowed city.
The poet Mary Ruefle writes whenever it

snows she wishes for someone to make love to—
all day in a bed of pale rumpled sheets,
blinds open to flake and shower. And it was like
that—the hurricane day for the storm that

never came. Friends came, and we drank bourbon
in our coffee. We kept the lights out as instructed,
lit candle after candle, burning our fingers
and having to suck on them like children. When

the friends went home, three floors up, we lay down
in bed like two good children. I touched
your face, mapping it finger-length at a time. How
utterly such moments get lost. You would be officially

diagnosed schizophrenic within the year. I would be living
on the other coast, wheeling a pram up the bare
California hills, saying to myself this is what
exile is—the world like a party full of strangers or

people you no longer wish to know. But if it all could
be held as under glass—as in those touristy plastic
domes you shake to make the synthetic flakes.
fall, knowing all the while it is really not cold in there,

just a cheap plastic toy filled with some chemical
version of salt water, and yet doesn't it give just the
tinest dizzying thrill? If it could all be held as under glass
I would pick that day. The promise of storm so freeing

I could admit everything that was wrong—with you,
with me, with us, our apartment of cardboard boxes,
unmatched dishes, half-bottles of alcohol, emptied
packs of cigarettes, even the death-music on the turn-

table, always someone singing about how to get lost or
more so, as if the expiration date was already stamped
on us, admit all this and think none of it mattered—
only the gloaming light over the skyscrapers, the

strange warm wind we walked out into toward evening,
finding sidewalks clotted with people like us, who had
waited all day for the hurricane, and now were dazzled,
smiling at the ordinary streets, which seemed at that moment

radiant, transfigured, the eye of everything.

And still the liquid moment spilling over cuffs, staining crook of
knees and elbows. *To use so thoroughly marks would be left.* Extra-credit
for desultory beauty? Or so we tended to think. Dumpster-smells
and foil-shined floors. The crusted window or musty lock. A
window falls and the hook turns. Savor of

regret like expensive wine. Kim died and left a scrawled note in
Lynn's book. Purer to me than any poem. Beautiful Lorraine so
often addled and/or bitter. I spread out the puzzle pieces and
arrange them by color. I

don't care about the final picture. Little patch of sky. Small moan
of smaller. How to get through the day without some minor
chemical infusion? We don't remember when we
last neglected to "watch ourselves." And still the liquid moment

spilling over cuffs,

.

"to use so thoroughly marks are left."

"bone-shine/ shiver,"

eleven mile island, hanging garden

map of what we wished

& didn't get

& what we did.

Turning Your Pillow to Find the Cool Side

Planets must cool, and even the hottest stars must
feel it inside them, a slight twinge, the molten
gases infinitesimally less so, and somewhere off
in the impossible distance—a distance that is
measured in million-mile columns of colored fire,
the threat of sheer space—the black alone. I knew
all along, I mean. I knew we spoke too easily, too
eagerly, the fire flickering over us from some location
we could not even see, the deepest space where
particles are born to collide, and who knows who,
who knows why, like turning your pillow to find
the cool side. Of course you retreated, subtly at first
and then in full flight—what skies do you wander?
How big are they and how do the lights appear at
the edge of the horizon? Even the stars can't abide
what lives in their bodies or how their ghosts journey
half-way across a universe to become the small
candles on a child's cake; you suck in your breath,
you make a wish and, one by one, they go out.

Marquee Moon

That song blasting out of my old boombox,
recorded from the radio, the fuzz level
too high, noises from the street
intruding persistently, but somehow
not distracting all that much and
Tom Verlaine, the strong-fingered hero,
plucking, playing and pounding
those long guitar solos that were almost,
but not quite, unendurable—

Just some song that played on and on—
nights watching cabs stream
through rain, and neon letters flicker,
vanish above the liquor store on the corner
where the beer was always almost
too cold to drink. And what somebody said
to me that summer about the horror
of dreaming—"like hearing voices
in your head, just out of reach,"
visions that give you a heavy weight
to keep bearing, and Tom Verlaine's fingers
dragging slow, as if that weight, too,
was his to carry.

Spectators Across the Interstate

The Camry was crumpled between a
Taurus and an Explorer—the Ford monopoly.
Somewhere in the middle, my sister had
tried to get out, purse flung wild—
reel of coins scattered across the interstate,
the blood gleam of pennies, bright thinness
of dimes, thick quarters; she was fine, and you
are waiting to hear this, curious like those who
followed us to the side of the road where we
waited for the ambulance. No blood,
no obvious bruising, just a crush in every bone,
a knowledge of the solitudes. The peanut
crowd, the gawkers so unsettling because
we were like them. We knew how close
someone must be for us to mourn, linking fingers,
the eight lanes of highway suddenly obscene—
such a rush, a roaring—what for? Queen Ann's
lace sprouted near a broken pipe that led
who knows where, pure smell of grass and
mint, among the tossed cans, the disposable.

What I Know of You

Bus stations in the dead hours
when the girls comb their hair in
the cracked mirrors of the four-
for-a-dollar booths that provide
backgrounds of Marilyn or Chuck
Norris and the junk sick hold
themselves like blown-glass
horses on a spinster's shelf.
Sunglasses and the morning paper,
the creased routines of rolled
tobacco and bare bread
and the glare of parking lots
at noon, like pews the shaded places
of loading docks and trans-national
trucks and the men who step out
and shade their eyes and the girls who
don't look at them and the women
who do, blue rivers of veins up
their thighs. And I would be drunk
like you on a log on a high river,
near the shore, but for a moment
off-kilter and afraid, as you right
yourself like the mercury in the level,
knowing at that moment
what is meant by float, to float on
this everyday sadness,
as the grapes float in the vat,

ferment into a holy red, which stains
the hands and feet of the harvesters,
the blind mouths waiting to be
blind.

Romance

I bought a cheap paperback on the stall
by the quai of Pont Neuf. Maxim Gorki's *Childhood*
in French, the dream-like pleasure of
reading a language half-apprehended—
so much I would miss and then the
small details striking like flint on
stone. Fires in the winter, the dark wood
dachas, the cart on the rutted frozen road.
An accident, blood spilled in the linden wood,
forests, where there were bodies buried,
abandoned from long seasons of war. And in
between the narrow shops I entered,
buying food that did not need to be prepared
or heated, wedges of hard cheese,
unripe apricots, the bread that staled on the
windowsill of my attic room. When I met
you that day on the street I had exhausted
those rituals of my aloneness. I broke the crusts
and let them fall, not even crumbs for
pigeons. I had forgotten even how to greet
those with whom I had some small contact—
the man who sold the Herald Tribune,
the shaved-headed girl behind the grille of
the metro station. No wonder when you took my
hand, touching your fingers to mine so briefly
I came undone. And later in that room, your body
unfolding like a kingdom, your hands so cold

they almost hurt, which only made me want
them more acutely as those passages of Gorki
gifted me obscurely with the sense that I
was entering a new country.

Thessaloniki

I meant to take photographs of the monuments:
Delos in the rain-light of autumn, the gusts of wind
from the vertiginous mountains where the snowlines
lay low across the villages, snow falling on the monasteries
where we stopped for metaxa and honey, and the
monks smelling of cold dirt, toothless, sharing the hard
bread, the yoghurt with cucumbers. If I had only known
I was happy, the wind on my face, Richard trying to put
his arm around me, the car with its heavy tires
groaning as it navigated the roads full of boulders.
In one town they unlocked the museum, a collection of
what the dead had left, small glass cups for tea,
platters of faded bronze, the thick velvet skirts and
waistcoats with their fraying embroidery. The camera to my
eye, I snapped Richard against a sky of violent clouds,
myself with a cigarette in a bathroom mirror. How
impoverished my dreams now seem. Drunk I kissed the
German hippie, walked with him to his hotel,
our bodies jutting against each other. I wanted it to
be a devotion, but we were both too drunk, too tired.
He said the name *Anselm Kiefer*. I said *the painter*.
He belched and rolled over to sleep. I crept out of
the bed before dawn, the streets of Thessaloniki shining
through their tarnish. Here the Turkish mosque, there
the café neon where the men drank *metrios* coffee and
ate plates of octopus. Below a port, the white ships
and the clouds darkening. Later, nursing a fearsome
headache I would see the beaten gold laurel crown of Philip
of Macedonia, the frail leaves, remnants of empire.

We misstate the word *frangible*,
able to be broken,
as sea-sponge, contents under
pressure, gel spilling
from a vitamin capsule.
The goodness leaking out—a waste,
but also the inverse, the capacity
to be penetrated by what
is *other*, the capacity
to shift, mutate. The sea sponge,
which swallows mouth after
mouthful of salt, even as stung
thirsts for more, the sponge wrung
dry, the brittle after, on sand
the honeycomb husk, almost weightless
in the hand, the wind of
this, which forms in the throat,
the need to keep speaking
even when not heard, the fracture
of such music, a note held
without pause, the old opera singer
trick of bending molecules,
nothing but a simple aria and
the glass breaks.

News of You

I learn to read you in the oily
silence of the lemons, a bowl
painted with chrysanthemum; in gray
November, a girl in a torn coat
sitting at the park bench staring at
her feet, the sexual cries of the
pigeons in the bean tree in my yard—
their flapping out at dawn, a flurry
of white like exposed thighs. Not
to listen for news of you as though
you had become a man in a book,
forever on page 243—entering a
room, softly closing a door. You
lift suitcases, pay the check,
the anonymous exchange of
quarters for coffee, a credit card
for a tank of gas. The tightness
eases but only in increments. So long
I spent snaring the trap—delicate
instrument of hair and wing, brightness
of blue bead and razor. Now if you
could only see me disassemble
it—how I struggle to love the
backwards glance, you changed into
mere figure—an illustration in my book
of illuminations: Boy with falcon,
holding out his thin wrists.

Barcelona

So many ways to be ruined. In the stone squares around
the Placa, discarded needles, a spray of blood,
the words of the murdered poet. Green like the wild
horses. A girl eats bread absently, crumbs falling
from her long fingers. A wounded pigeon hops on one
leg. The stones themselves are pitted, scarred
here. When the revolution ends, men hold stones
in their mouths to stop them from speaking. Never
enough wine or bread no matter how often it
is multiplied. In the church, the crooked child wishes
to be something else. A length of smooth wood,
a stick that would help someone walk or beat
a man with a sound like wind. Cruelty sprouts in
the slender weeds between the cobblestones. Anything
better than to be always crushed this way. We, too,
came here hungry. Brandy and coffee in the cheap
cafes, so many cigarettes our throats ached in
the mornings. What was dying between us briefly
lovely—a respite from our seasons of slow bickering.
In the cathedral, built like a child's dribbled sandcastle,
the slashes of light in the darkness, saying there would
be an *after*, saying we would get through this, and
the stairway with its warm smell of piss and sour wine,
where we climbed into the bleaching light, where we
understood what it would be to be forgotten.

Poem for Thule

If I call you *calamity* I keep circling this
same field where you are not. And yet perhaps
that is where the damage opens, as the wound
opens to whatever is inside it. Pus and blood,
the leaking out, which could be in some world—
if not this one—a trope for belonging. You
will guess what I am trying to do: find a way to
rename you I can believe in, so I am not merely *here*,
scrabbling amid stones. This weekend, I planted
all for myself a garden, spread the manure on the
seedlings, that smell—rich and almost unpleasant
of used life. I thought every one would die, but
they did not, even though for a whole week I neglected
to water them. If I neglect you this way what does
it mean that you keep returning? I have given up the
notion of recompense—stranded in how to live
between. Yet like a vapor or mist I still rename
you for myself *the beautiful thing*, invent a
location where you hold me as a magnet
pins pure north—tundra where the icy forms
linger—pristine, unchanging, the remnants of
every explorer, their packaged meals and sextants,
scrawled journals of what they missed, even
the apple core, emerging from the ice as if new-
minted, smelling of orchards.

& how you make me more alive

In the high plains, the bright colors of
buildings in snow

I see only a picture on a screen

myself turning away
(this long and studied) fading of even the idea

You (us)

For so long I wanted you
It was not (pretty) though I willed it so

it was (not) but every time you
walked in a room

a small foretaste like two children on
a boat

shining (and) stillness

the voices hushed for night like the house

where the father walks around
turning (out) the lights

or the tiny frogs croaking in the mud basins

what pulsing of throat what (open)

I practice imagining you in places I can't see

from (tiny) pictures reconstruct elaborate
daily routines

what stones you count, two ravens on a wire
fence or

six swans aligned on a nickel-colored lake

even a sourness of local bread
(do they eat bread?)

local rice, the cold in the bowl
the thin pancake. It doesn't matter (any) more

he plays more beautifully when she is gone

The orphic (the Orpheus) lute player

 in an after of river and willow

heedless and lost (where) his fingers find
the edge in the string

I read this in the "Dictionary of Myths," a book

I love for its quixotic title. The muffle (echo)

voice through the trees (which is this)
in which I keep pruning (back), cutting lines

like threads of wire as though (without) them I

would (sing) better or (fly)

Orpheus, the Late Years

Not true that he became resigned
or that the small moments
were any kind of comfort; yet it was
the small things he noticed,
the details striking him so vividly now
in the gloaming. He loved to watch
the orchards, the plums, the pears—
that cycle of insipid blossom
so quickly followed by the florid fruit.
This was an aria he knew, but
it was in winter that he knelt against
the stones and beat his fists
against the earth as a drum. Winter—
black branches, a gleam of
ice, the trees a twilight body
lit by diamond, rolling star, even the
light more lucent now that it had
nothing to deflect it, sifting down
through the naked branches. Her
body as he remembered it—sweat
and sting, the last time, when he
could hide nothing from her any longer,
when she saw him as he was and
fate forced her eyes away. Death
stripping them back to the beginning
of each other, the blossom white and
star-shaped, the blossom veined in green,
shining and so easily crushable.

Numinous

Today driving to work across Solano,
a wide and ugly street of Sonics
and used car lots, pay-by-the-month appliance
stores and all the motley messy details
of daily life in the fifth poorest statistical
metropolitan cluster in our nation, I glanced
down at the slim white scar on my wrist,
and for a moment I could not remember how
it had gotten there. The usual story: the razor
the bathtub, the failure to cut in the right
place or the right direction, the discovery,
the shame, the emergency room, the friend,
the psychiatrist, the little two-tone pills—pink and
blue, yellow and red with names like
Ambien or Zoloft, *all better now*, their
stated mission; and though I could bring back
all this so clearly, I could not remember
what had led me there, not the actual steps
but the inner logic, the burning wire, the me-
that-wanted-to die. It was in Vermont, snow
blocked the roads, blanketing the churchyard,
which I loved, with its uneven graves of hands,
fingers crooked like St. John the Divine in the painting
in the Louvre attributed to Leonardo, the hands
almost concealed under thick white crusts
like so many half-sandwiches given up to the slate
sky. Mark Lyon took me there. The days I wasted,

believing myself so in love with him that nothing
was better than pacing through that longing. I cannot
remember that either. I now inhabit the world
of the mother, changed, reduced as sauce is reduced
to the hunk of meat, the tender bone. I care only
for what will keep the fire stoked, engines rolling.
And that white scar, it shimmers like some kind of
Hollywood heaven. What a fool I was, how little
I knew, etcetera, etcetera.

What to Wear

I dress you in leaves so you will feel the trees' waiting.
What it is to be vulnerable to any drift of wind.
I dress you in water so you know how to dance, how
to fall and tap and break and reassemble. Today I
make you a shirt of nettles, pants of thorns so you
will be prepared for the worst. Tomorrow, a cloak of
feathers, a pillow of down. I sew you blankets of
seedpod and husk, eggshell and nest so you know
what it is to miss something, to feel abruptly
emptied. I stitch you robes of petals and berries,
staining your hands when you put them on, staining
your body so you will know the meaning of plenty.
Good, good enough—the grass–woven sandals, the
bark suit. I give you a loom so you learn how to work
it—mending, erasing, building the fine cloth.
Yet perhaps this is my mistake, for afterwards you
believe only that everything should be whole, clean,
tight-woven. Now I am the one who does not
know what to do. I dress myself in a suit of mud.
I dress myself in a suit of moss. These wash away
too soon, and I find myself naked among the willow
and tamarisk, beside the river, whose voice I use
to call out for you, though you don't answer, though I
wish only to ask you what it is I should wear.

Overcoat

The past recedes further. We still wore clothes from the
forties then, antiques, but the thread still strong,
the buttons still hooked to the cloth. Until I saw the man
in the tweed coat, its faint unraveling around the hem,
I had forgotten how we looked as I have forgotten so many
other details. Your Irish tweed coat with its horn buttons
and grains of tobacco in the pocket, coffee stains down one
sleeve from when you rushed catch the Number 1 train most
mornings. How was it ever possible I thought we could make
any kind of life? Your hand shakes even in my remembering.
You cut yourself shaving, so reckless, later you looked like a
boxer after a hard round. I touched the frayed hem at
your wrist as we crossed Claremont. That empty apartment
any painter would have loved for its light. The blued shell
of morning lifting around us. Coffee and half-and-half, tinfoil
wrapped cubes of bouillon like little bon-bons, a meal if
there was nothing else to be had. Love dies—that is what
I have learned. You would not believe how completely it
vanishes from the body—the emptied banks of memory except
for this rare intrusion, the coat of the strange man creased against
his shoulder blades. We were not happy; we should not have
stayed together. Yet is it not odd how in retrospect pain
shines like pleasure—a subtle, voluptuous light.

Letter in October

The man holds himself still in the
glaze of wisteria, that purple bruise
cool to enter me. Now he walks across
s sunlit plaza, the doves above, the
familiar background—drill, paint thinner,
a stillness in his bones and mine—
October: The trees preparing to flame
and fall, become the bareness
under us. I walk to my classroom down
a hall hushed with dust, blown up
from the south, the pure desert where the
light might pin him, leave him
without so much as a shadow.
And today I am all cage, the bones
holding barely, the lava inside corrosive,
a terrible bloom. *Want me*, the hum
my pulse spins when I know it means
so little—shiny thread, bright button.
Doves gather on the branches outside,
plum petals shiver to ground, the burn
inside the tree, the chill it senses under
the flitter of sunlight, blue and more blue,
the sky like an intercession.

The Dead

Villon said snows of *last* year not yesteryear. The dirty secret
of organic farming, the peach grower in the Willamette Valley
told me: the fish blood on the fields. The necessity
of it—bone meal, the dried flakes of skin. If I could live
with the notion of perfection, but like Tennyson, I keep
wanting the you-as-you-were, the gray patch in your hair,
your need to keep drinking past the point when it was
amusing. In a review of Milton, James Woods writes
the lovely thing is how Adam and Eve rescue themselves—
Adam could have been immortal, forever, in the garden,
the glass-voiced God willing to press the rewind button,
pluck another rib, forge an entirely new woman. Yet Adam,
chooses instead to wander—to be the mouth of dust,
the footprint erased. And so nights I roam the blood-
fields, the bones spread across like tiny cilia feeders.

Prescription for After

What I assume I know is your aloneness,
which is only—naturally—the reflection of
my own. Little film of us on the darkened street,
the klieg lights silenced, the soundtrack
muted. I used to be so afraid of the silent old
films my parents made me watch. *Isn't it funny?*
they'd say of Charlie Chapin trying to eat
his shoe. I could only see his mouth moving
desperate. I could only imagine myself with
leather between my teeth. This is the sensation
I have, these days, when I see you. Walking
across some boring plaza perhaps or down a
hallway carpeted with blue industrial speckled
squares. Or not boring: the world—the sycamores
and cherry trees all blood-red and gold, and
birds sectoring the sky like a musical score.
Your aloneness *not mine*, not the same as mine.
That is the one truth of it, what I read in this
October chill, the air darkening the mornings,
and the rush when I start the car, my own breath
suddenly visible, finite, precious, if not to you.

These days I go by the name of ____

"Love should not have to be a murder," you tell me.
For days I ponder what you mean. Behind every story
another, each word shutting out what might be.
When I loved you, I said it was because you knew
how to chainsaw a cord of wood, fix our creaky
woodstove, read the calls of the birds hidden in
the far pines. Sometimes I don't know if you are
that person anymore—or if I am, the one who
waited at the end of the logging trail all afternoon
while you climbed to the peak. *Love should not
have to be a murder*, but too often it is. We
cling to history as to a string of beads—each
one counting down, *this* and then *this*. These days
I go by the name of *what-would-I-save-if-the-
house-was-burning*. These days I go by the name
of *too-much-water-under-the-*. And yet the
strange sweetness of some mornings—a mist above
the frozen grass, the Vs of ducks travelling miles
for a split of water. Perhaps the only name worth
having is *do-over*—or the notion of the story
you tell; each time you change it just slightly:
The girl opens the door to fetch the water. The girl
rides the donkey. An arrow flies through the trees.
The fairy tales I tell our children all have this one
thing in common—the forest is large as is the world,
the child goes out and no one knows where
the path will lead. Love should not have to be a

murder. These days I go by the name of *the-path-not*. These days I go by the name of *wet-leaves-on-the-windows*, the name of *here-are-the-bright-ghosts-in-all-we-see*.

How to Influence Dreams

I have held you as close as a cat the color of
smoke. Not your fault you are dangerous.
Not your fault your eyes are the color of steel
in rain, or that you make me think so often
of roads and hail, suitcases and busted locks,
a sprig of mustard flower in early morning,
the world peeling itself back like a ripe beach.
Not your fault you fill me like a wind,
so I burn the toast and batter the windows
shut until the children begin to quarrel and weep.
I have burned sage through all the rooms,
locked my doors against you—though I
still dream you at odd moments. You flit
around the side of the house, you are some
wild thing and even the traps laid with peanut
butter and honey will not hold you. You are the
mass of doves that scoot out from the bean
tree, the blossoms that fall and redden
from the bushes of the pomegranate. Like
the sweet wild plum, you are best held in
memory. Not your fault that you can't
help clawing at the furniture. Not your fault
that you fill the empty chair at every
table I set. I try to gift you with what I have—
the plates of tomatoes sliced with basil on top,
the steaming cups of tea or soup. Nothing works.
You keep being as hungry as ever. I am trying

to teach us both to sit here at the table—bare
as it is, to sit here in this kitchen blue with
morning. Somehow, the two of us, we will find
a way to love what we have.

Fifty

You may come to a place where your
life thins out, almost unrecognizable, this
yard of cracked ice, and the muffled sounds
of the doves in the bush; they will fly
out at you like darkness, a chilling
inside, the layers that seal you from what
you know. You pick up the nuts from the
ground and turn them in your hands. At
a remove you call them lovely, little cradles
sealed around the withered meat. And yet
the waters still flood, a seasonal occurrence.
And today in the ankle-deep, strange
birds alight as if emerging from air,
the long travelers—the swallows, the
finches, the golden warblers.

Post Millennium

(for Duncan)

We could talk about what is small, meaning hard.
the odd corners the broom doesn't reach,
that fist of clean straw, notion of sluice,
nets of black widow, the dust balls that
catch the bread crumbs, burnt matchsticks,
the sticky ends of popsicles, whatever you don't
want to see. Us in the parking lot of the
supermarket with our bleeding chops.
In the Payless, in the K-Mart. We could talk
about what we need. I could give you a glass of
cold tap water, watch you drink it, each flex of
muscle in your throat, which I associate with
beat, this depleted music of everyday. Confess
how once we rehearsed such heroics, picture
the climatic saga moments—the wolf at the door,
the burning house from which we haul the naked child.
I could tell you how artificial watermelon makes me
desperate as does "tropical sunset" when used as a name
for a scent. Describe how as children my sister and
I drank honeysuckle from the bush at the bottom
of the garden, not knowing how hard and long,
how rare to be holy. You and I at the dinner table,
drinking our thin coffee, moving around each other
so carefully because to pin it down would be to lose
the blue-edged shadow that is all we cling to.
Instead, I give you this glass of plain water. I give
you the dust that rests on it.

Acknowledgments

Many thanks to the editors who first published these poems, often in earlier forms, in the publications below:

"Broken World" in *In Our Own Words: A Generation Defining Itself* (anthology), 2004; "Garden" and "Black Hope" in *Poemeleon*; "Broken English" in *WomenWriters.Net*; "Las Dos Fridas or Script for the Erased" in *Wordgathering*; "First Love," "The Readers," "Overcoat," "Muse," and "Prescription for After" in *VLP Magazine*; "Goodwill" in *Naugatuck River Review*; "At the Embajada" in *Tattoo Highway*; "Icon" and "Fifty" in *Lingerpost*; "Nocturne Avenue D" in *How to be a Maquiladora* (chapbook), Main Street Rag Publishers. 2007;"This Slow Ache Within Music, and "Thessaloniki" in *The Salt River Review*, "Wen Kroy" in *Superstition Review*, "Little Grief" in *Din*; "Hurricane Day" in *Sweet*; "Turning Your Pillow to Find the Cool Side" and "These Days I go by the Name of____" in *Weave*; "Romance" and "What I Know of You" in *Valparaiso Poetry Review*; "Getting Over the Fear of Form," "Ghost Time," "Spectators Across the Interstate," "Numinous," "Estrangement," and "Recovering (2)" in *Diode*; "News of You" in *Cutbank*; "Barcelona" in The *Innisfree Poetry Journal*; "Poem for Thule" in *Blackbox Manifold*; "& how you make me more alive" and "Letter in October" in *Talking Writing*. "Orpheus, the Late Years" in *Caesura*;"What to Wear" in *Owl Eye Review*. "How to Influence Dreams" in *Adobe Walls*; "Post-Millennium" in *Tidal Basin Review*.

For their help and friendship many thanks to Louis Asekoff, Jennifer Bartlett, Robert Boswell, Rus Bradburd, Kara Dorris, Andrew Fenton, Amy Silin Freas, Michelle Granger, Jen Habel, Tony Hoagland, Craig Holden, Kevin Honold, Melissa Kwasny, Dana Kroos, Allison Layfield, Philip Levine, Michele Marcoux, Candice Morrow, Antonya Nelson, Marnie Nixon, Denise Ondayko, Michael Northen, Bernadette Smith, Megan Snedden, Joseph Somoza, Carrie Tafolla, Stephanie Taylor, Lynne Thermann, Dick Thomas, Michelle Valverde, Joseph and Sofie Vastano, Connie Voisine, Joni Wallace, Amanda Ward, George Ypsilantis, my parents, Clay and Moira, sisters, Samantha and Sarah and my husband, Duncan Hayse. I would also like to thank my son, Walker Hayse.

About the Author

Sheila Black is the author of *House of Bone* and *Love/Iraq* (both CW Press). She co-edited with Jennifer Bartlett and Mike Northen *Beauty is a Verb: The New Poetry of Disability* (Cinco Puntos Press), named a 2012 Notable Book for Adults by the American Library Association (ALA). In 2012, she received a Witter Bynner Fellowship, for which she was selected by Philip Levine. She lives in San Antonio, Texas where she directs Gemini Ink, a literary arts center.

Other Orphic Prize winners still available from Dream Horse Press:

American Amen by Gary L. McDowell

Galley of the Beloved in Torment by Kyle McCord

Disloyal Yo-Yo by Bruce Cohen

The Martini Diet by Gaylord Brewer

Body Tapestries by S. D. Lishan

Baiting the Void by Penelope Scambly Schott

Please visit our website for more information:

www.dreamhorsepress.com

CPSIA information can be obtained at www.ICGtesting.com
Printed in the USA
LVOW11s0350180614

390375LV00003B/48/P